D1829290

Fifty-Six

The stories behind the fifty-six men of World War II remembered on Abingdon's War Memorial (plus other heroes who are not!)

Steve King

Copyright © 2020 Steve King

All rights reserved, including the right to reproduce this book, or portions thereof in any form. No part of this text may be reproduced, transmitted, downloaded, decompiled, reverse engineered, or stored, in any form or introduced into any information storage and retrieval system, in any form or by any means, whether electronic or mechanical without the express written permission of the author.

The views expressed in this work are solely those of the author and do not necessarily reflect the views of the publisher, and the publisher hereby disclaims any responsibility for them.

ISBN: 978-0-244-86255-8

PublishNation
www.publishnation.co.uk

Author's Preface

The inspiration for my book came out of a conversation I had with my late uncle Eric in the spring of 2013 when he was ninety-two years old, - so what did you do in the war then Eric?

"I was a sergeant in the Northamptonshire yeomanry, it was a tank regiment, went over to Normandy with the invasion, in a landing craft with a barrage balloon above and towing a piece of the Mulberry harbour behind. Went through the battle of Caen, then headed north to Paris, then through Belgium and Holland until we reached the Rhine. We crossed the Nijmegen - the bridge too far. After the armistice I stayed in Holland for a year until I was de-mobbed." Blimey, we never knew this - did you get any medals? *"Never bothered to apply for them."*

Without him knowing, we applied and got his medals which we presented to him that summer, but on condition he wore them at the coming Remembrance Sunday Service at the town's memorial. After that service he asked if he could read the names on the memorial. Tearfully he recalled some of those listed: *"See the Rutty Boys? Went to school with them. That chap there, sat next to him. That one was my best mate and so on.*

Sadly, two months later Eric and his memories passed away. How could I not perpetuate their stories?

Eric Henry McIntyre, B.E.M.

My mission was to explore the circumstances behind each of the fifty-six men listed on Abingdon's war memorial, but it didn't end there. There are three, Thomas, Jakeman, and Williams who are from Abingdon and are buried in Commonwealth War graves in Abingdon cemeteries, but are not listed on the memorial. Also, to investigate the dozen or so men who are buried in CWGC graves in Abingdon cemeteries who, although not listed on the memorial, have military links to the town, mostly via RAF Abingdon?

Methodology? Given there is little first-hand knowledge still available, my research has been very much based on existing documents, however, where evidence is sometimes inconsistent, even contradictory, I've used a methodology of "more likely" or "most probably" in deciding what an outcome or scenario might be. My findings are by no means definitive, and I have written this with the best of intentions, while accepting there may be some errors. If you discover any inaccuracies then do contact me so as I can make amends.

A huge thank you to staff and researchers at the Commonwealth War Graves Commission (CWGC); The Imperial War Museum (IWM); St Andrews College, Oxford; The Royal Berkshire Regiment museum (The Wardrobe); Oxfordshire C.C Coroners & Registrar Office; Air Crew Remembered; Midland Aircraft Recovery Group; The Map Archives; Abingdon School; Abingdon Library; CS Wiggins; Jackie Smith; Bob Goodenough; and, of course, my long suffering wife, Daphne.

Introduction

June 4th 1940 with the evacuation of the B.E.F from the beaches of Dunkirk almost complete and most of Europe as we know it under the tyranny of the Nazi Fascist movement, Great Britain stood alone. Adolf Hitler had offered a negotiated, peaceful surrender option to G.B, and the response was one of the greatest speeches of all time. In parliament, Prime Minister Winston Churchill took to the floor and said:

"Even though large tracts of Europe and many old and famous States have fallen or may fall into the grip of the Gestapo and all the odious apparatus of Nazi rule, we shall not flag or fail. We shall go on to the end, we shall fight in France, we shall fight on the seas and oceans, we shall fight with growing confidence and growing strength in the air, we shall defend our Island, whatever the cost may be, we shall fight on the beaches, we shall fight on the landing grounds, we shall fight in the fields and in the streets, we shall fight in the hills; we shall never surrender, and even if, which I do not for a moment believe, this Island or a large part of it were subjugated and starving, then our Empire beyond the seas, armed and guarded by the British Fleet, would carry on the struggle, until, in God's good time, the New World, with all its power and might, steps forth to the rescue and the liberation of the old."

That said, Hitler prepared for the invasion of Britain. Meanwhile, P.M. Churchill ordered the creation of Special Operations Executive (S.O.E.) and tasked Hugh Dalton "to get on with it." On the 22nd of July, Dalton confirmed to the P.M that S.O.E was now in existence, to which the P.M replied, *"Good and now go and set Europe ablaze."* And do that he did.

S.O.E. made contact with resistance organisations throughout Europe, supplied and trained them. S.O.E operatives (spies) were dropped behind the lines, and commandoes and "others" carried out the most daring of raids, the epitome of such was the numerous Norwegian resistance raids on the Third Reich's ambitions of producing a nuclear bomb! After the humiliating Commando raid on St Nazaire, Hitler, incandescent with rage, sent this "Kommandobefehl" (Commando) order to his Generals:

"Henceforth, all enemy troops encountered by German troops during so called commando operations, though they appear to be troops in uniform or demolition groups armed or unarmed, are to be exterminated to the last man. If such men appear to be about to surrender, no quarter should be given."

Officers were required to submit a daily report on the numbers liquidated, and the order, once digested, was to be destroyed so that no written evidence of this breach of the Geneva Convention could ever be produced in court as evidence of war crimes. However, toward the end of the war, a high-ranking officer was arrested in Germany and was found to have the only surviving copy hidden in the lining of his coat.

That order was to have severe consequences for resistance fighter and allied troops, not least, dare I suggest, for at least five men featured here.

Chapter One

The Army

Barge, Peter F. Driver 1942605 of the 185 Tunnelling Company, The Royal Engineers, died 28th of April 1942 age 19. Son of Herbert & Eileen Barge he is buried in the Bedlay Cemetery, Lanarkshire. I cannot find the cause of his death? The 185 tunnelling comp was one of the most famous of WW1 and reformed at Scarborough in 1941, moving to Falkirk later in the year to continue their training programme. They took no part in any front line action during WW2 and later disbanded. Apparently much of their records were lost in a fire during the Blitz?

Belcher, Percy, Pte 5333831 of the Army catering Corps attached to the 4th battalion, The Royal Berkshire Regiment died May 9th 1942 age 29. After the 4th Royal Berks were all but wiped out at Dunkirk the remnants of the Battalion was stationed on the Isle of Thanet, Kent which was also home to RAF Manston as well as the ports of Ramsgate, Margate and Dover all of which made the area a prime target for the Luftwaffe. At the time of his death the Nazi's launched Operation Baedeker, which was a concerted effort on specific targets rather than indiscriminate blanket bombing. The idea was to destroy buildings and infrastructure in an attempt to lower moral and the spirit of the civilian population, Thanet took a particular, almost nightly pounding through the months of April & May and it is believed Pte Belcher was killed in one such raid? Pte P Belcher is buried at Abingdon Cemetery.

Belcher, William Edward, Sapper 14398672 of 3 Bomb Disposal Company. The Royal Engineers, died on the 22nd of March 1945 (seven weeks prior to V.E Day) age 36, son of Edward & Mary Belcher of Abingdon. Originally based in Nottingham 5 BDC crossed to Normandy on the 5th of July 1944 landing at Arromanches, they took up base at Coulombs, France from where they supported the invasion force. Sapper Belcher, K.I.A, is buried at Abingdon Cemetery.

Bint, William Thomas, Corp 5336144 of the 56th Reconnaissance Corps died in Tunisia on the 25th of November 1942, age 24.Son of William & Louisa Bint of Abingdon. Corp Bint is buried along with 2,524 Commonwealth Servicemen at the Medjez-El-Bab Cemetery, Tunisia. Ahead of ground forces, the 56th Recce Corps was known as the eyes and ears of the Army. On November 16th the 78th Division pushed out crossing the Atlas Mountains ahead of "Blade Force", the 1st Army's spearhead which comprised of 6 Armoured Divisions, tanks from the 17/21 Lancers, motorised company of 10 Rifle Brigade, a Squadron of the Derbyshire Yeomanry Armoured Cars, 1 Para, a Battery of 25 pounders (RHA) a Battery of Anti-Tank Guns, a Troop of Bofors and a troop of Sappers. At the forefront of this mighty force? The 56th Recce Corps with Corporal Thomas Bint who is listed as K.I.A.

Belcher, Raymond Charles, Lieutenant 258144 of the 6th Airborne Recognisance Corps died on the 6th of June 1944 (D-Day) age 20 and is buried at the Ranville CWGC Cemetery. Lieutenant Belcher is the son of B.C Belcher and in 1940 was house prefect at Brighton College, his address was "The Cottage, Abingdon. Berks.

"Operation Tonga" was in some respects the prelude to operation "Overlord" the invasion main. Late on the night of the 5th of June Lieutenant Belcher made the crossing by glider, possibly from RAF Harwell, towed by aircraft from 620 sqn from near-by RAF Fairford. Crash landing at 03.35 hrs, he certainly would have been one of the first to land in Normandy, his objective was to establish H.Q and as Lieutenant in the Recognisance Corps would have been the eyes and ears of the following invasion. Sadly he would have been one the first casualties of the invasion too. (Please refer to the Kommandobefehl order in my Introduction.)

Ranville CWGC cemetery contains 2,236 Commonwealth burials, 90 of whom are unknown.

Ranville was also the first village/town in France to be liberated when members of the 6th Airborne, along with the 7th Parachute regiment arrived either by parachute or glider in the early hours of June 6th.

This is the burial certificate for Lieutenant Belcher together with the name of the pilot and crew of 620 Sqn who never made it back!

(398) Dd2855/WtP1471 20,000 (2) 11/53 JC&S Gp669

MKM

Graves Registration Report Form.

COUNTRY: FRANCE
XXCOMMUNE:

REPORT No.: SCHEDULE No.: 190

PLACE OF BURIAL: RANVILLE WAR CEMETERY

Land belongs to

The following are buried here:—

Certified complete and correct.

Signature ~~~ Records Dept, France Date 3 JAN 1955

PxBxGx	No. and Rank		Initials, Name & Honours		Unit	Date of Death	For works use
Gr.No.			PLOT VIA, ROW C				
	176884	P/O (Pilot)	A.H.	BARTON	620 Sqdn. R.A.F.(V.R.)	6.6.44	C.H
	258144	Lt.	R.C.	BELCHER	6th Airborne Armoured Recce Regt., Recce Corps, R.A.C.	6.6.44	C.H
	1550834 ɸ	F/Sgt. (Nav.)	H.M.	BITTINER	620 Sqdn. R.A.F.(V.R.)	6.6.44	C.H JEW
	14405006	Pte.	G.	COPSON	7th Bn. Parachute Regt., Army Air Corps	6.6.44	C.H
Coll. 1-25	1894261	Sgt. (F/Eng.)	G.	CROSSE	620 Sqdn. R.A.F.(V.R.)	6.6.44	C.H
	7947393	Tpr.	M.P.	DONE	6th Airborne Armoured Recce Regt., Recce Corps, R.A.C.	6.6.44	C.H
	420192	Cpl.	P.T.	EARWICKER	6th Airborne Armoured Recce Regt., Recce Corps, R.A.C.	6.6.44	C.H
	6354955	Pte.	R.A.E.	FRANCIS	7th Bn. Parachute Regt., Army Air Corps	6.6.44	C.H
	14420431	Pte.	V.P.C.	FROST	7th Bn. Parachute Regt., Army Air Corps	6.6.44	C.H
	4343281	L/Cpl.	J.	GASCOIGNE	7th Bn. Parachute Regt., Army Air Corps	6.6.44	C.H.

ɸ Authy: RA/1/3 dated 23.12.54

14

Branson, Henry James, Private 13021189 of the Argyll & Southerland Highlanders died on the 10th of January 1942 in Malaya, age 26, son of William & Kate Branson and husband of Edith of Abingdon. Early in the Malayan campaign the Argyll's countered the invading Japanese forces, while heavily outnumbered they inflicted such casualties on the Japanese 5th Infantry Division that the enemy brought in the Imperial Guards. On January the 7th at the Slim River Japanese brought up their tanks and motorised infantry, but by now the Argyll's were exhausted and severely depleted. Decimated, only 94 managed to return to British lines. Private Branson is buried at the GWGC Cemetery, Taiping, Malaya where 864 Commonwealth Service men are buried, 500 of whom are unidentified.

Burborough, Rex, Private 5110473 of the 1st /7th Royal Warwickshire Regiment died on the 13th of July 1944 age 21, son of William & Lucy Burborough of New Northcourt, Abingdon. The 1st /7th Royal Warwickshire's came ashore on the 6th of June (D-Day) at Sword beach and immediately began the task of pushing back the enemy. The 1st/7th were particularly involved with taking Caen and the Calvados area from the Germans in what was called operation Epsom. Pte Burborough is buried in the Ryes Cemetery, Calvados, along with 596 Commonwealth Servicemen.

Dix, Arthur Earnest, corporal 14357864 of the Royal Army Medical Corps died 20th of August 1945 age 29, son of James and Louise from Tubney, Abingdon. Curiously Cpl Dix was re-buried to the Cologne Southern Cemetery in 1947. The last battle in Cologne was in March 45 when the city finally fell to a US Tank regiment, not long after that Germany capitulated, but Cpl Dix "died" some months after the surrender and given his grave registration states he was not classed as K.I.A (killed in action) but as "died". I can only assume he became ill or had an accident after war ended?

Downing, Sydney John, Lieutenant 245353 of the 7th London Rifle Brigade died on 3rd of June 1944 age 20 at Monte Casino, Italy, son of John & Barbara Downing of Abingdon. Monte Casino was one of the most bitterly contested locations in WW2 and arguably the most contested of all during the Italian Campaign. Although the 7th was originally an infantry brigade it morphed very quickly into a mechanised one with tanks and an array or armoured vehicles. Lieutenant Downing is remembered on the Dragon School, Oxford, Roll of honour where he is listed as "Killed in Action" he is buried at the Monte Casino CWGC cemetery.

Gawthorne, Arthur Joseph. Pte 7630926 of the Royal Ordinance Corps, husband of Marguerite Lillian Gawthorne of Abingdon died on the 7th of October 1940. The Royal Ordinance Corps was responsible for the supply and maintenance of weapons, munitions and vehicles and operated from bases/camps throughout the country, although I can find no place of death and this was at the height of the Blitz here, was he killed in an air raid? Pte Gawthorne is buried at Abingdon cemetery.

Gibbens, Thomas Mervyn, Sergeant 5335418 of the 6th battalion, The Black Watch, Son of Joseph & Helen Gibbens of Abingdon died on the 14th of May 1944 age 33 at Monte Casino, Italy. Soldier Helps of the Black Watch recalled. "*Our battalion of 1001 men advanced onto Monte Casino, but three days of fighting reduced us to 97. Imagine how I felt talking to a comrade, then turning round to see him wounded, or worse. Or when, as one group of nine men, with two or three meters between each of us, only three were capable of movement after* *the area had been bombarded with German shells. I was lucky to only have a shrapnel wound"* Sergeant Gibbens is buried at the Monte Casino CWGC cemetery.

Hounslow, Eric Frank, Private 5337650 of the South Lancashire Regiment died on the 14th of October 1944 age 23, son of Mr & Mrs W G Hounslow of Abingdon. Shortly after Operation Market Garden (AKA Arnhem) the South Lancs were involved in heavy fighting with the enemy in and around the drop zone, but their main objective was to relieve the 1st Airborne Division and the Polish 1st Independent Parachute Brigade who had become completely surrounded by the enemy at the two bridges across the Rhine they were trying to secure.
In their attempt to establish a land route to the bridge at Nijmegen the South Lancs along with the Para's and Polish forces took heavy casualties, including Pte Hounslow, who, with 662 Commonwealth and Allied Soldiers is buried at the CWGC cemetery, Mierlo, Holland. (Please refer to the Kommandobefehl order in my Introduction.)

Hart, Harry, Private 5393225 of the 5th Battalion, the Hampshire Regiment son of Arthur & Ellen Hart of Abingdon. K.I.A. on the 16th of September 1943 age 31 at Salerno,
On 3 September 1943 the Allies invaded the Italian mainland, the invasion coinciding with an armistice made with the Italians who then re-entered the war on the Allied side. Commonwealth and American forces (Private Hart among them) landed on the beach near Salerno on 8-9 September 1943, there was fierce fighting for some days in and around the bridgehead they had established. Private Hart was among the many K.I.A during the battle. He is buried at the CWGC cemetery, Salerno.

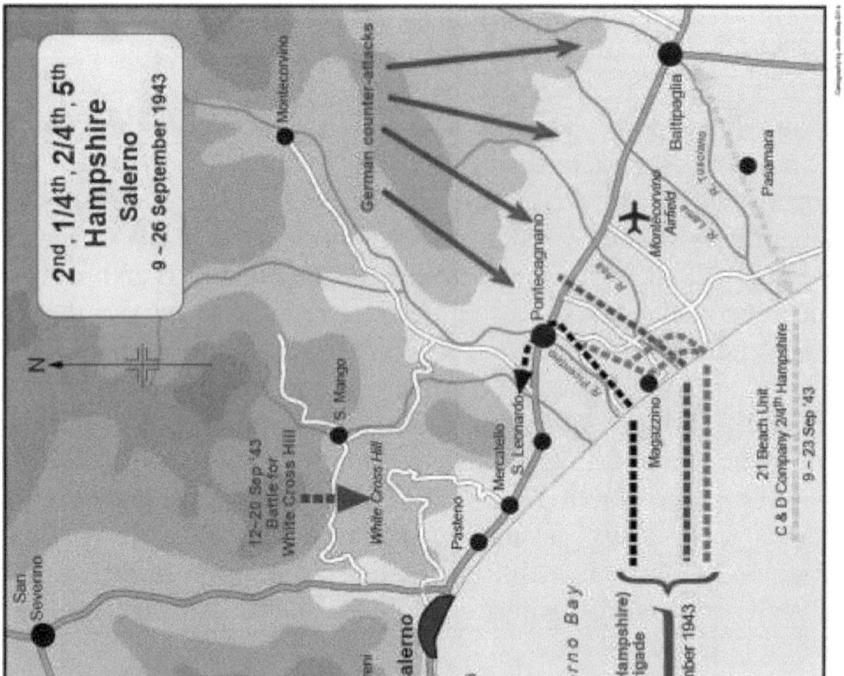
2nd, 1/4th, 2/4th, 5th Hampshire
Salerno
9 - 26 September 1943
Legend
7th Armoured Division
128th (Hampshire) Brigade
2nd Hampshire
1/4th Hampshire
5th Hampshire
2/4th Hampshire
German counter-attacks
Montecorvino
San Severino
Nocera
Camerelle
S. Marino
San Lucia
26 Sep '43
Cava Cemetery
Cava de Tirreni
25 Sep '43
Vietri
Salerno
Pastena
Mercatello
S. Leonardo
S. Mango
12-20 Sep '43
Battle for
White Cross Hill
White Cross Hill
Pontecagnano
Magazzino
Montecorvino Airfield
Battipaglia
Pasamara
Salerno Bay
128th (Hampshire) Brigade
9 September 1943
21 Beach Unit
C & D Company 2/4th Hampshire
9 - 23 Sep '43
Minori
Maiori
Amalfi
Naples 15M
Captured
1 October '43
ITALY
0 1 2 3 4 5 Miles

Hudson, Harry William, Gunner 969818 of the 60th Field Regiment, The Royal Artillery died at El-Alamein on the 12th of December 1941 age 22, son of Harry & May Hudson, wife of Violet. After regrouping from their evacuation of Dunkirk the previous year and having spent most of the summer fighting in Iraq the 60th Field regiment arrived in Egypt in September 1941 and became part of the 7th Armoured Division of the Eight Army, "The Dessert Rats". In November they crossed the border from Egypt into Libya as part of Operation Crusader and on the 21st they mounted an attack to relive the garrison at Tobruk. However, they came under a fierce attack not only from daily raids by Stuka dive bombers but from Rommel's Afrika Corps, for three days the 60th was at the forefront of the battle against two Panzer Divisions. Many were killed or taken prisoner and most of their guns were put out of action. Gnr Hudson, K.I.A and is remembered on the El-Alamein Memorial.

James, J - An Enigma? As with all my research my first port of call is the CWGC who list some 40 or more James .J. deaths between 1939 & 1946, researching these I find none with any affinity to Abingdon? Next I researched each of the 433 James (omitting the J) listed as Army fatalities, but again I fail to find one with any Abingdon connection, however, I found 10 without affinity to any location? Supplying the CWGC with the relevant service numbers they confirm through their next of kin data that neither of those ten had any affinity to Abingdon either? Parish registers and the registrar's office confirm no matching deaths too. However, The Brookwood Memorial in Surrey lists & remembers over 3000 "personnel" who died during the conflict, but for one reason or another their bodies were never found, among those listed are members of the resistance, Commandos on special operations, spies, allied personnel operating under alias's and several S.O.E operatives.

There is listed a Jones, John, L/Cpl of the Royal Corps of Military Police whose date of death is given as 17th of January 1946, some six months after V.E day? But the MP were at that time peace keeping in Palestine and Israel. St Andrews college Oxford have a vast archive on this subject at that time, but they confirm no Jones J as far as they know, served with the MP there? The R.C of M.P archives have no record of him serving with them either but went on to suggest S.O.E operatives were sometimes given a regiment as cover? S.O.E was disbanded soon after the surrender (summer 1945) but it is documented that a few were "unofficially" kept on to track down and capture Nazi war criminals. Regimental records, local newspaper archives and even the War Memorial Trust appear to have no record of a James J. from Abingdon who died in WW2 while serving in the army? Which begs the question was James. J an S.O.E. Nazi hunter?

Quite by accident I discover that pretty much anyone could nominate pretty much anyone to be included/recorded on a memorial, therefore I can only assume a local person (relative, ex-employer or even an old acquaintance) who at some point knew James. J nominated him to be included on Abingdon's memorial? For sure he is one of the 433 Army personal listed by the CWGC, but quite which one is a complete mystery?

Janes, Edwin Ivor, 5251033 Private, the 1st Battalion, the Royal Worcester's died on the 28th of November 1941 age 21. Son of Cyril & Florence Janes of Abingdon. The main battle for North Africa began on April 10th 1941 with the Royal Worcester's positioned around the Halfaya area of Egypt where for the next fourteen months they fought a bitter battle against Rommel's Afrika Corps, until on the 21st June 1942, surrounded, beleaguered and depleted the entire regiment surrendered. However, the regiment was reformed and re armed in 1944. Pte Janes, K.I.A. is buried at the Halfaya Sollum War cemetery.

Kelly, Patrick Joseph, Gunner 1094237, the 125th Anti-Tank Regiment, the Royal Artillery died approximately on 15th of June 1943, age 31, "somewhere along the Burma Railway" Son of Michael & Sarah and husband of Nora of Abingdon. In order to supply their forces along the Malayan Peninsular and beyond the Japanese embarked on building the notorious "Burma Railway". Using almost entirely forced labour from Commonwealth, Dutch and American prisoners of war, work began in June 1942 and ended some eighteen months later in December 1943. The death railway claimed the lives of 13,000 prisoners who were systematically beaten and starved to death, at one time when 300 came down with sickness they were killed, their bodies burned. Burial records show Gunner Kelly's date of death is given as "approx." After war had ended his body was discovered and recovered from an open grave alongside the railway and reburied in the Kanchanaburi Military Cemetery, Thailand.

Leslie. Roy, Private 1804087 of the 14th Battalion the Sherwood Foresters died at Anzio on the 21st of May 1944 age 22, son of Frederick & Violet Leslie of Abingdon. Victory in North Africa meant the allies could launch an attack on the enemy by landing in mainland Europe. September 1943 the first allied troops landed in Southern Italy. The Sherwood Foresters were among the first ashore at Anzio in January 1944 in an attempt to out flank the Germans. In May the Foresters finally broke out of their beach head and made for Rome which was captured on 3rd June, just two weeks after Pte Leslie was K.I.A. He is buried at the Beach Head War cemetery, Anzio, Italy.

Lindsay, Jack, Gunner 1543452 of 78 Battery, 38 Lt AA Regiment. The Royal Artillery died on the 9th of September 1945 in the Lintang Japanese P.O.W camp, Sabah, Borneo age 45. Son of Jack & Jane Lindsay and Nephew of Mrs Harris of Abingdon. Written elsewhere here are the facts about the fate of the 80,000 British, Commonwealth and Allied service men and women along with several thousand civilians who were taken prisoner by the Japanese after the fall of Singapore. It is impossible to recreate in anyone's mind the savagery and in-humane way in which these unfortunate souls suffered at the hands of the Japanese, but on the 30th of August 1945 Japanese Commander of the camps, Suga told the prisoners news of the Japanese surrender, however the camp was not liberated until about the 12th of September (some three days after Gunner Jack Lindsay's death) and in those dozen or so days the Japanese garrison embarked on an orgy of violence beyond comprehension. This is the account of interned civilian nurse, Hilda Bates, who throughout her capture did her best to comfort and care for the POWs.

"I was horrified to see the condition of some of the men, I was pretty well hardened to sickness, dirt and disease, but never had I seen anything like this in all my years of nursing. Shells of men lay on the floor sunken eyed and helpless, some swollen with hunger, oedema, and beriberi, others in the last stages of dysentery lay unconscious and dying. No pillows or clothes, a few cups, a fewer bowls. There were three hundred sick men unable to help themselves or to carry food too their mouths. Throughout our internment the women of the camp asked to tend to the sick and dying, but the Japanese refused saying it would be indecent to do so."

It is incomprehensible to imagine what Gnr Lindsay endured during those years as a prisoner, or the circumstances surrounding his death? Rightfully In 1947 Gunner Jack Lindsay's body was exhumed from the Lintang P.O.W cemetery and laid to rest at the CWGC cemetery, Labaun, Malaya.

Mills. Douglas Edward, 2nd Lieutenant 138400 of the 31st Field Regiment. The Royal Artillery was K.I.A. in Keren, Eretria on 18th of February 1941 age 23, son of Percy & Cicely Mills of Abingdon, he is buried at the Keren War cemetery, Eretria, N Africa. Keren was the last Italian stronghold in Eritrea and the scene of the most decisive battle of the war in East Africa during February and March 1941. Guarding the entrance from the western plains to the Eritrean plateau, the only road passing through a deep gorge with precipitous and well-fortified mountains on either side, Keren formed a perfect defensive position. On these heights the Italians concentrated some 23,000 riflemen, together with a large number of well sited guns and mortars. After ten days of gruelling combat the Commonwealth troops succeeded in forcing their way through the seemingly impregnable defences on the ridge and finally through the 200-metre-long road block which the Italians had blasted at the narrowest point in the pass. Keren was taken on 27 March. The defeated Italian force retreated in some disarray to Asmara, which fell to Commonwealth forces on 1 April, and the Italian surrender was taken at the port of Massawa on 8 April 1941

Pimm, David, Trooper 7945648 of the 9th Queens Royal Lancers died at San Savino, Italy on the 5th September 1944 age 24, son of David & Agnes Pimm of Abingdon. Trooper Pimm, K.I.A, is buried at the Gradara War Cemetery. Italy. One of the oldest regiments the 9th Lancers were originally a cavalry regiment but by the time of WW2 had become a mechanised force with a variety of armoured vehicles including Sherman tanks, On 3 September 1943 the Allies invaded the Italian mainland, the invasion coinciding with an armistice made with the Italians who then re-entered the war on the Allied side. Following the fall of Rome to the Allies in June 1944, the German retreat was based on a series of defensive positions known as the Trasimene, Arezzo, Arno and Gothic Lines. The 9th Lancers landed in Italy in 1944 and in September of that year were in action at San Savino in what was known as the battle of the Gothic line, a Nazi defensive line stretching inland from the Adriatic Coast. With others including Canadians the line was broke enabling the Allies to continue pushing north.

Proctor, Leslie, Gunner 1062103 of 78 Battery, 35 LT Anti-Aircraft, Royal Artillery died on the 12th of August 1945 in Indonesia age 37. The 78th HQ was in Oxford with many of its men drawn from the local community's (and somewhat older than most) Embarkation was December 1941 reaching Singapore on 13th January 1942, however it was not possible to hold back the invading Japanese who overran the Peninsular and captured some 80,000 Allied troops. The 78th were transferred to a POW camp in Borneo where they fared better than other POW camps until the beginning of 1945 when malnutrition and disease began to set in, then deaths took place rapidly, even past VJ day to the extent that of all the men who were captured and sent to Borneo, none returned. So ended the tragic story and history of the 35th LT AA Regiment, Royal Artillery.

Sanford, George, Sergeant 5336178 of the 9th Battalion the Parachute Regiment K.I.A on the 5th of January 1945 in the Village of Bure, Belgium, age 23, son of George & Esther Sanford of Abingdon. Sgt Sanford is buried in the only war grave at "ON" communal cemetery, Luxemburg (Belgium) The German offensive through the Ardennes forest of December

1944, (more commonly known as the Battle of the Bulge) lead to the urgent dispatch of the 6th Airborne Division to Belgium. On the 29th December, the Division was ordered to advance against the German front, during the 3rd to the 5th of January they became embroiled in incredibly hard fighting around the village of Bure, but succeeded taking the village and held it thereafter against fierce counterattacks, however, in so doing suffered sixty-eight dead and one hundred and twenty-one wounded or missing. Often where but a single serviceman is buried in a communal cemetery suggests they were operating alone and behind lines? (Please refer to the Kommandobefehl order in my Introduction.)

Short, Arthur Albert, Pte 5339032 of the 4th Battalion. The Royal Berkshire Regiment, son of William & Fanny Short and husband to Violet of Abingdon, K.I.A. on the 22nd of February 1942 age 41. Given the 4th Battalion were based on the Isle of Thanet I'm assuming he died in one of the many air raids to that area? (See details of such with Pte P Belcher) Pte Short is buried at Abingdon cemetery.

Webb, Charles Reginald, Lance Corporal 5336765 of the 1st Battalion, the Queens Own Royal West Kent Regiment (the Buffs) K.I.A. on the 9th of November 1944 age 24 at Meldola, Italy. The son of Charles & May Webb of Abingdon, L/Cpl Webb is buried at the Meldola War Cemetery along with 143 UK soldiers who were also K.I.A that month alone. With Allied forces well established in Italy the push northwards taking on a variety of German defensive lines began, by August 1944 the Germans had withdrawn from Florence and Rome and the 1st Battalion had moved across to the Adriatic sector where they were involved in heavy fighting while attempting to cross the Savio river and establish a bridgehead and it was during this action L/Cpl Webb was K.I.A.

Wicks, James Macrae Corrie, M.C. Major 64611 of the 1st Battalion, The Hampshire Regiment died on the 12th of June 1944 (D+6) in the Bocage, Normandy, only son of Reginald & Eleanor Wicks of Park Rd, Abingdon. Major "Jimmy" Wicks, M.C is buried at the Hottot-les-Bagues cemetery, Calvados. He left Winchester College for Sandhurst in 1933 and was commissioned in 1935, joining the 1st battalion in India in 1936, soon promoted to Lieutenant, the battalion left for Palestine in 1938 to undertake peace keeping duties.

From Palestine he went to Egypt to round up Italians after Italy declared war, from there the 1st were taken to Malta to defend the island from imminent air and seaborne invasion. Eventually returning to Palestine he was given a temporary position as Major and later Lieutenant-Colonel. He was mentioned in dispatches in 1943 and then returned to England with the 1st battalion and practised assault landings in preparation for D-Day.

He was officer commanding Support Company on "Jig Green" sector of Gold Beach, the first wave ashore was approximately 0730 but came under heavy fire from a German strong point that had survived the "softening up" barrage from the Royal Navy.

As expected there were heavy allied casualties not helped by the fact strong winds had blown their landing craft much further east than planned? Wicks organised all into a fighting force and although wounded led the force off the beach and inland to the village of Asnelles where again he led the force in liberating the village and capturing 25 prisoners. For this action he was awarded the Military Cross. On the 10th of June the 1st Hampshire's advanced through the Bocage and south of Bayeux where they came up against well organised, stiff opposition which halted their progress. On the 12th the 1st tried once more to advance and it was in this action while charging on a machine gun post ahead of his men, he was killed.

Major James Macrae Corrie Wicks MC

Lieutenant Raymond Charles Belcher

Chapter Two

Operation Dynamo (Dunkirk)

During May 1940 Abingdon lost SEVEN men covering the retreat of the British Expeditionary Force (BEF) to Dunkirk and the eventual evacuation off the beaches by sea back to England. Known as Operation Dynamo where a requisitioned armada of 600 "Little Ships" along with ships of the Royal and Merchant Navy rescued a staggering 338k men, sadly some 30k soldiers fighting a rear-guard action covering the retreat did not make that evacuation. Listed as K.I.A (killed in action) or taken prisoner, they warranted a separate dedication here.

The 4th Battalion, The Royal Berkshire Regiment landed in France in January 1940 and became part of the 8th infantry brigade, the B.E.F. In March they left for Belgium and took up defensive positions arounds the Gementee Woods. On the 17th they were ordered to withdraw and passed through Brussels en-route to defend the Albert Canal.

During this period the battalion was locked in bitter fighting all the way until finally reaching their objective (Dunkirk) in May where they were over powered and over-run by the Nazis. The majority of the Battalion were either killed or captured, those captured remained P.O.W's for the duration of the war. The remnants (about 80 of the original 800) of the 4th Battalion were evacuated off the beach at Dunkirk on the 31st of May.

Operation Dynamo, the Plan

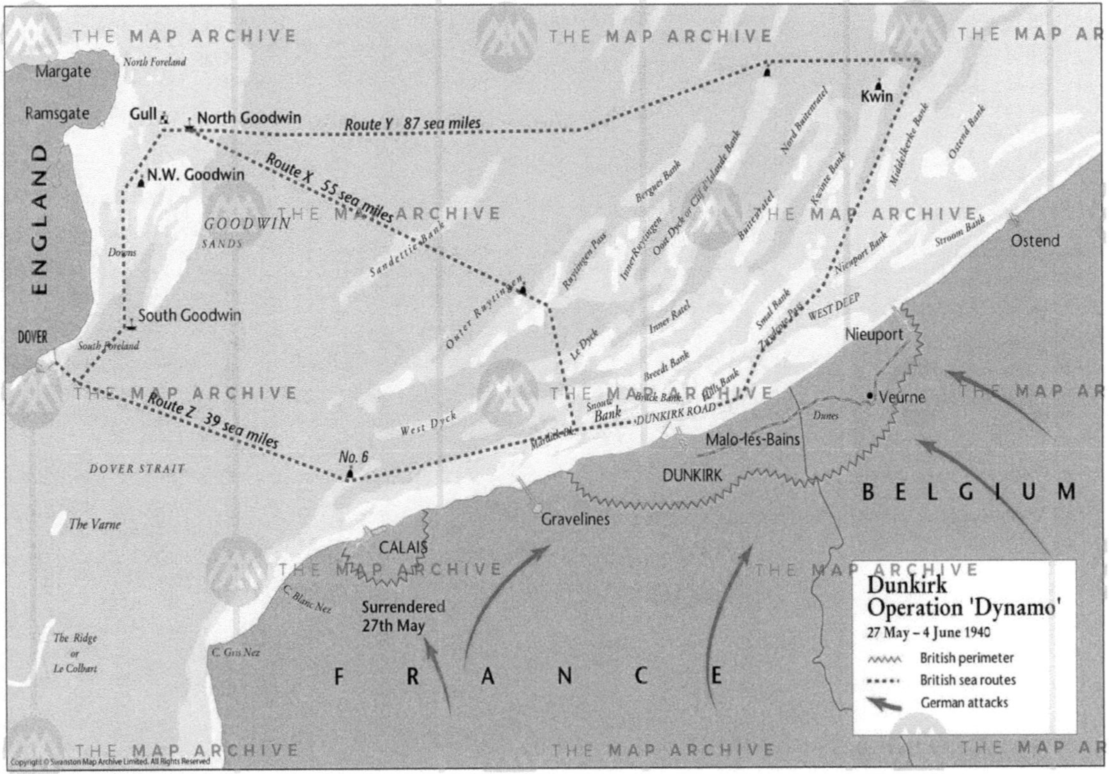

THE MAP ARCHIVE
Copyright © Swanston Map Archive Limited. All Rights Reserved

Copyright, the Map Archives

The evacuation began on 26th May, 1940, Route Z was the shortest route at 39 miles but could only be used at night because of German artillery from mainland France. Route X at 55 miles was dangerous because of sand banks and our own mines. Route Y at 87 miles was the longest but easiest to navigate and least risky and was much favoured.

As many as possible of the rear-guard soldiers were picked up on the 1st & 2nd of June with another flotilla taking place on the 3rd to rescue 26,000 French troops fighting a rear guard action before Dunkirk finally fell on the 4th of June 1944.

Requisitioned "Little Ships" of the Thames on their way to rescue troops from Dunkirk

The Beach Head at Dunkirk

Copyright, Getty images/The Guardian

Bedworth, Charles, Lance Sergeant 5377501 of the 4th Battalion. The Royal Berkshire Regiment K.I.A on the 21st of May 1941 age 19. Son of Earnest & Daisy. L/S Bedworth was K.I.A while taking part in the rear guard action covering the retreat of the British Expeditionary Force (B.E.F.) to Dunkirk. He is buried at the St Ledger Church Yard Cemetery, Hanaut, Belgium. L/S Bedworth "Almost made it home."

Lee, Reginald Percival, Private 5336463 of the 4th Battalion the Royal Berkshire Regiment K.I.A. covering the retreat to Dunkirk in Belgium on the 29th of May 1940 age 22, the son of Richard & Winifred Lee of Abingdon. Pte Lee is buried at the Zuidschote Cemetery, Belguim. Pte Lee "Almost made it home."

Marsh, Henry John, Private 5333164 of the 4th Battalion, The Royal Berkshire Regiment K.I.A. near Dunkirk on the 24/05/1940 age 29, Pte Marsh was covering the retreat of the B.E.F, son of Henry and Ivy, Husband of Ann of Abingdon. Pte Marsh is buried in the Dunkirk cemetery. Pte Marsh "Almost made it home."

Rutty, Lewis Bernard, Private 5337644 of the 4th Battalion, The Royal Berkshire Regiment, died on the 10/05/1940 age 20, son of Henry and Elizabeth Rutty of Abingdon, K.I.A covering the retreat and is buried at Zuidschote Church Yard, Belgium.

Rutty, Leslie Henry, Private 5337661 of the 4th Battalion, The Royal Berkshire Regiment, K.I.A on the beach at Dunkirk on the 1/06/1940 age 21, Brother of Lewis above Pte Rutty is buried at Veurne Cemetery, Belgium. The Rutty boys "Almost made it home."

Bennett, Albert Earnest, Private 5110890 of the 2nd battalion The Royal Worcestshire Regiment K.I.A. on the 30th of May 1940, age 22 son of Lillian Hart of Abingdon died on the beaches of Dunkirk and buried at the Wulverdinghe Cemetery, Belgium. Pte Bennett "Almost made it home."

Howe, Roy Victor, Sergeant 5330384 of the 1st battalion the Oxford & Buckinghamshire Light Infantry (Ox & Bucks L I) died at Dunkirk on the 20th of May 1940 age 39, husband of Winfred Howe of Abingdon. He is remembered on the Dunkirk memorial. On the 17th of May the 1st Bat, Ox & Bucks L.I. moved through the forests of Seignies to cover the retreating B.E F from the overwhelming superiority of the advancing Nazi's. The 330,000 men of the B.E.F were making their way to Dunkirk in the hope of being evacuated to England. After holding their position through the night, they were ordered to march 26 miles (under fire) to Zavelberg and join other forces retreating to Dunkirk. On two occasions the 1st held off desperate attempts by the Nazi's to breakthrough their line. On the 30th of May the remnants of the 1st finally reached the beach head and the only pier, the Mole. Alongside was HMS Worcester and the Merchant ship Maid of Orleans, meanwhile further along the beach the requisitioned "little ship" Sundowner, skippered by its 66-year-old owner Charles Herbert Lightoller and his 18-year-old son Roger were picking up troops off the beach. Nine officers and 320 NCO's of the Ox & Bucks L.I. boarded the ships and made it back to England, Incredibly, 175 of them crammed onto Sundowner who then delivered its cargo safely back to Ramsgate while zig-zagging to miss attacking enemy aircraft. Sgt Howe "Almost made it home."

Students from John Mason School, Abingdon, including my Granddaughter, laying a wreath and poppy crosses for each of our fallen on the Dunkirk Memorial July 2019.

A Soldier's Prayer

Lord hold our troops in your loving hands.
Protect them as they protect us.
Bless them and their families for the selfless acts they perform for us in our time of need.
Amen.

Anon.

Chapter Three

The Royal Navy

Brightman, Benjamin, FAA/SFX684 of the Fleet Air Arm, Royal Navy, died on the 15/11/1942 age 23, son of Benjamin and Daisy Brightman, husband of Joyce Brightman of Abingdon, Berks. Benjamin served upon HMS Avenger which was a one-time U.S. Navy war ship converted into a "Flat Top" (aircraft carrier) his ship was torpedoed and sunk with heavy casualties near Gibraltar by German submarine U-155. With the sea as his grave Benjamin was buried at sea and is remembered on the Lee-on-Solent Fleet Air Arm Memorial.

Writing to the Admiralty, Lieutenant Commander N. F. Kingscote, Commanding Officer of the near-by HMS ULSTER MONARCH, wrote:

"At 0315, a vivid reddish flash appeared on the Starboard side of AVENGER stretching the whole length of the ship and lasting for about 2 seconds. This flash made a perfect silhouette of the ship, and was followed by a pall of black smoke - After the flash, nothing more was seen of AVENGER but one or two small twinkling lights were observed in the water, obviously from floats. H.M.S. ULSTER MONARCH passed over the position of AVENGER within 3 minutes and nothing was seen...."

Brightman, Stuart, Ordinary Seaman P/JX631943 died on the 22/08/1944 age 18, son of B and F D Brightman of Abingdon, Berks. O/S Brightman served on H M S Bickerton, a U.S built

Frigate and at that time was part of an escort group guarding the carriers H M S Trumpeter and H M S Nabob who in turn were covering convoy JW-59 en-route to Russia, at about 0100 hrs they were discovered by enemy submarine U-354 who first launched a torpedo against H M S Nabob and badly damaged her, at 01.22 hrs a second torpedo was Fired at H M S Nabob but missed and hit H M S Bickerton which resulted in 40 fatalities. She was eventually scuttled by a torpedo fired from HMS Vigilant. With the sea as his grave O/S Brightman is remembered on the Portsmouth Naval memorial.

HMS Bickerton on fire and about to be scuttled

IWM

D'Almaine, R, Harry Robert, Lieutenant Royal Navy, died on 13/05/1941 age 25, son of Harry George W and Edith Sophia D'Almaine, nee Horsepool and husband of Margareta D'Almaine, nee Thame. Lieutenant D'Almaine served on H M Submarine Undaunted, she carried out her first patrol from Malta at the beginning of May 1941 and was deployed off Tripoli. An attack carried out by Italian warships and aircraft preparing to attack a departing convoy to Trapani on the 12/05/1941 is believed to have caused her sinking, but there is also speculation she may have hit a mine? With the sea as his grave Lieutenant D'Almaine is also remembered on the Portsmouth Naval Memorial and was mentioned in dispatches!

HMS Submarine "Undaunted"

IWM

NB, Abingdon School lists:- Private Roy D'Almaine, 1896 – 1916, Canadian infantry (Alberta Regiment) killed in action in France on 04/11/1916 age 20, son of HGW D'Almaine of the Square, Abingdon, Berks, Roy attended Abingdon School from 1906 to 1909. Is this Lieutenant D'Almaine's grandfather?

Hemmings, Kenneth, W R, Ordinary Seaman P/JX21543 died on the 05/12/1940, son of William and Kate Hemmings of Abingdon, Berks. O/S Hemmings served at HMS Excellent which was a training establishment in Portsmouth, 1940 was the beginning of the Blitz (and the battle of Britain) and Portsmouth was particularly singled out because of its naval importance.

One of the first "city-wide" air raids on Portsmouth took place on December the 5th (the day of Kenneth's death) there were 40 reported fatalities and about 140 casualties, based on this information it is probable that Kenneth was among those forty fatalities killed in the air raid? He is buried at Abingdon Cemetery.

Hoey, Patrick John, Leading Seaman P/JX149552 died on 20/07/1941, L/S Hoey served upon HMS Umpire, a brand new Submarine which sank in collision with an HMS Trawler just nine days after commissioning while en-route to joining the fleet. L/S Hoey has the sea as his grave and also is remembered on the Portsmouth Royal Navy Memorial.

Junior officer Edward young's account of the sinking:

"The sea continued to pour in on us, as the level crept up on the starboard side the electrics began spitting venomously, vaguely I wondered if we would all be electrocuted, in the half-darkness men became anonymous groping figures, but there was no panic. I discovered a man trying to open a water tight door that I had just shut "my pals in there" it's no good she's filled right up and there's no-one left alive on the other side, he turned away sobbing a little"

Cold, shivering and in darkness, Young made his way to the conning tower where he and three of his ship mates squeezed in, thinking anyone able would have already made their escape through the engine room hatch. They closed the hatch and began to flood the vessel in order to equalize the pressure, only when the conning tower was flooded were they able to open the outer hatch and make their escape! Of the crew, 16 escaped, but 22 were lost.

Paul, Cyril James, Leading Seaman P/JX382198 died on the 14/12/1944 age 20, son of Fred and Rose Paul of Abingdon, Berks. L/S Paul was killed when his ship H M S Aldenham struck a mine and sunk in the Adriatic Sea.

HMS Aldenham was a type 111 Escort Destroyer "Hunt Class" she is credited with sinking U boat U-587 on 9th of March 1942 and after circumnavigating Africa was ordered to join the Mediterranean fleet escorting convoys between Malta and Tobruk, from there she took part in the invasions of Salerno and Anzio before being assigned to the Adriatic where in support of the Yugoslavian partisans she hit the mine and sunk, 63 of her crew were rescued, sadly 126 and 2 partisans were lost. She was the last Royal Navy Destroyer to be lost in WW2. With the sea for his grave he is also remembered on the Portsmouth Memorial.

Allison, George Edwin, PO/X1753 of No 41 Commando, The Royal Marines, K.I.A. on 15/06/1945 age 30, son of Albert and Gertrude Allison and husband of Monica Allison. Commando Allison is buried at Reichswald Forrest war cemetery, Germany. (Please refer to the Kommandobefehl order in my Introduction.)

41 Commando was part of the Special Service Brigade that landed on Sword Beach on June 6th 1944 (D-Day) from there they fought their way through France, Belgium, Holland and into Germany where they took up occupation duties until eventually being disbanded in January 1946. Reichswald Forest War Cemetery was created after the Second World War had ended when the bodies of servicemen from all over western Germany were brought to this, the largest Commonwealth Cemetery in this country.

Some were members of land forces moving through the forest, others died crossing the Rhine, among them too are members of the 6th Airborne Division (Operation Market Garden) and a good deal are airmen who "came down" during the numerous operations over occupied Europe. There are 7,594 Commonwealth Servicemen buried or commemorated here as well as 78 "other nationalities" mostly Polish

Smith, Peter William, Supply Assistant P/MX71663 died on the 24/05/1941 age 19, son of Stanley and Sybil Smith of Abingdon, Berks. S/A Smith served on H M S Hood, (affectionately known as the Mighty Hood) and went down with his ship, he is remembered on the Abingdon War Memorial as well as the Portsmouth Naval Memorial.

The Mighty Hood, pride of the British Fleet

The Bismark firing on HMS Hood taken from the bridge of the Prince Eugene

Chapter Four

The Sinking of HMS Hood and the Bismark

The Royal Navy had been tasked to find the German battleships "Bismark" and "Prince Eugen". H M S Hood (laid down in 1916) and the very new Battleship H M S Prince of Wales intercepted the enemy ships in the Denmark Straight at 0535 on the 24/05/1941, with the Hood opening fire at 0553. Anxious to join the battle fast approaching H M S Norfolk (uncle's ship) however, for the Hood it was all over in seconds. She took several direct hits causing major fires to break out, unfortunately one was in the ammunition hold which subsequently blew its magazine in spectacular fashion. The mighty Hood rolled and sunk taking all but three of her 1,418 crew with her!

The Prince of Wales also took some direct hits, one to the bridge killing all in it bar one, she subsequently broke off the engagement leaving Norfolk to shadow and harass Bismark. However, Bismark didn't escape unharmed, she was hit at least once damaging her fuel tanks, her fuel was then contaminated by sea water and she'd also lost a large amount of oil, her speed was significantly reduced. Determined to avenge the sinking of the Hood, Norfolk shadowed the two German ships, but the slowing Bismark was in need of repairs and headed for the French Port of Saint Nazaire leaving the unscathed Prince Eugen free to attack Atlantic convoys. Churchill ordered "sink the Bismark" clearly the admiralty were about to throw every asset they had to carry out those orders. The chase was on!

Norfolk was joined by H M S Suffolk, then the H M S King George V and then H M S Rodney, next morning along with H M S Renown and H M S Dorsetshire they closed on Bismark and began to shell her, fresh to the hunt were the aircraft carriers H M S Victorious and H M S Ark Royal and a torpedo from one of the attacking aircraft hit and jammed Bismarks rudder. That night a flotilla of cruisers arrived comprising of H M S Cossack, H M S Maori, H M S Piorun, H M S Sikh and H M S Zulu and immediately took over shelling the Bismark. By morning she was low in the water, listing heavily and on fire when her crew deliberately scuttled her! Two days after the sinking of the Hood the Royal Navy (and Mr & Mrs Smith) got their revenge! S.A. Smith is remembered on the Abingdon War memorial

The fleet closing in on the Bismark,

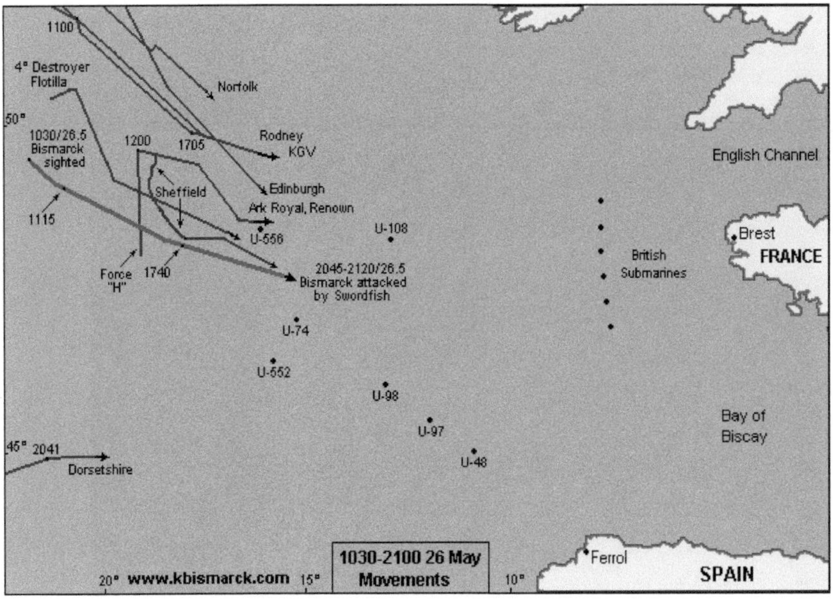

The Sailor's Hymn

For those in peril on the sea,

Eternal father strong to save,

Whose arm hath bound the restless wave,

Who bidd'st the mighty ocean deep,

Its own appointed limits keep,

Oh, hear us when we cry to thee,

For those in peril on the sea.

William Whiting

Chapter Five

The Royal Air Force

Andrews, George Victor, Sergeant (wireless op/air gunner) 1181372 of 18 Sqn the Royal Air Force Volunteer Reserve, died on 17/11/1942 age 22, son of James and Grace Andrews of Abingdon, Berks. Sergeant Andrews is buried in Massicault War cemetery, Tunisia.

Using Blenheim Medium Bombers the Sqn flew to Malta in 1941 where they took part in raids against enemy shipping, but by January 1942 they were down to just five aircraft and withdrew to Egypt. From there it was reformed with new aircraft and personnel mainly in support of ground forces through Algeria, Tunisia, Sicily and finally Italy.

On the date of his death he took part in a low level formation attack on the Bizerta airfield taking advantage of the low cloud forecast, but en-route the mission was to be abandoned because of insufficient cloud cover, however, some of the aircraft, led by Wing Commander Malcom continued to the target, two of those aircraft were lost when they collided and a third was shot down, the rest returned safely. Sergeant Andrews is buried along with four other members of 18 Sqn (most likely his crew mates) who died on the same day?

Barrett, Dennis Charles, Flying Officer 75922 of 211 Sqn, the Royal Air Force Volunteer Reserve, died on 02/01/1941 age 25, son of Richard and Eileen Barrett of Croydon Surrey.

He is buried in Phaleron Cemetery, Greece. Flying Blenheim Medium Bombers 211 sqn took part in operations against the Italians in Libya and the Western Dessert, but after the invasion of Greece (via Albania) by the Italians in October 1940 the Sqn was sent to support that country against its invaders. Records state F/O Barrett died as the result of a car crash in the early hours of New Year's Day 1941

Blenheim Medium Bomber

Bennett, Herbert Bapume, A.C.1 620296 of 13 OTU unit (training) was based at RAF Bicester and was the husband of Edith May Bennett of Abingdon. he died on the 10th of June 1940 aged 23 while on board Fairey Battle aircraft that was involved in a flying accident, his crew mates, Flt Lt (pilot) Alan Chalmers and AC2 Samuel Davis were also killed.

A.C 1 Bennett is buried in a CWGC war grave at Abingdon Cemetery. His wife's message reads:

"MY DARLING HUSBAND HUBERT
KILLED IN A FLYING ACCIDENT.
SWEET REST HAS FOLLOWED PAIN
WE HOPE IN GOD WE MEET AGAIN"

Bernthall, Leslie Lawton, Flight Sergeant 1165008 of 70 Sqdn, the Royal Air Force Volunteer Reserve, died on 08/07/1943 age 22, son of James and A L Bernthall of Abingdon, Berks.

He is remembered on the El-Alamein memorial where more than 3,000 Commonwealth airmen with no known grave are listed on the R.A.F panel. 70 Sqn was a bomber squadron operating Wellington aircraft across North Africa, the Mediterranean and the Middle East and at the time of his death the squadron was used as front-line support to Montgomery's 8th Army. Flt Sgt Bernthall and his crew were in Wellington HF 752 when it was lost.

Nb, A Mr & Mrs Bernthall of Abingdon placed an advert in the 2nd of August 1940 edition of the North Berks Herald appealing for information relating to their son Cyril, who was reported is missing in action on the 24th of May (which was the time of Dunkirk) thankfully I can find no such individual being killed and believe him to have been taken as a P.O.W.

Davies, Roy, Aircraftman 2nd class, 914885 of the Royal Air Force Volunteer Reserve died on the 21/03/1944 age 23, son of William and Matilda Davies and husband of Elsie Davies of Saxton Road, Abingdon, Berks.

A/C Davies is buried in Ramleh cemetery, Israel. I can find no trace of any aircraft lost on that date, however at that time there was much conflict between Israel and Palestine as well as continuous terrorist activity too, I'm assuming AC Davies was killed during such (as reported in the North Berks herald). The cemetery contains the graves of 1,168 Commonwealth personnel who died in Israel and Palestine.

Ellison, Henry Victor, Flight Lieutenant of the Royal Air Force Volunteer Reserve died on the 24/03/1942 age 44. The husband of Wynfrid Dodson Ellison of Abingdon, Berks. He is remembered on the Singapore Memorial which stands in Kranji War cemetery and bears the names of more than 24,000 Commonwealth casualties who died during the campaigns of Malaya and Indonesia and have no known grave, among the casualties listed are airmen who perished over the seas and land. The battle for Singapore & Malaysia began in January 1941 and ended with the battle for Singapore on the 15th of February 1942 with some 80,000 allied service men and women taken prisoner by the Japanese. About that time Flt/Ltn Ellison post was given as being as in "administration and special duties"? The prisoners fate at the hands of the Japanese was worse than can be possibly imagined, those who were classed as fit were put to work on projects like the Burma death railway and those who were not were simply starved to death or bayonetted where they fell. Mindful that Flt/Lt Ellison's date of death is given a month after the fall of Singapore one can only assume he was captured before or on the fall, but somehow met his fate at the hands of the Japanese soon after?

Foy, Thomas Joseph, Flight Sergeant (air gunner) 1313948 of 83 "Pathfinder" Sqn, the Royal Air Force Volunteer Reserve died on 06/08/1944 age 22, son of Thomas and Gladys Foy of Abingdon, Berks. He is buried at the Pontoise Communal Cemetery, France.

83 Squadron was a bomber squadron flying Lancaster Mk 1 & Mk2 aircraft, (among there officers was a young Guy Gibson who transferred to 617 "Dambuster" squadron) In spring of 1944 the squadron transferred to R.A.F Coningsby and became a stand-alone Pathfinder squadron employing only the best of the best in the RAF, leading the way deep over enemy held

territory to identify and mark out with flares the chosen targets for the following bombers. Flight Sergeant Foy's Lancaster ND 930 (Q-Queenie) was shot down by enemy fighters on the return leg after identifying and attacking the V1 Rocket Storage site at Bois de Casson. Their Lancaster came down near Pointoise where he and his seven crew mates are buried.

On that raid Lancaster ND 930 (the pathfinder) was accompanied by Lancaster's W 4824, PB 140, ND 840 and LW546 - W4824 "crashed" over France, ND 840 was brought down by flack, PB 140 was "beat up" so badly some of the crew bailed out over France, but the aircraft somehow continued homeward, however, thinking all was lost.

W/O Lester of the RAAF chose to bail out over the English Channel (his body was recovered from the sea later) but still the aircraft continued homeward until eventually what was left of its crew managed to crash land over Sussex!

More curious is the fate of Lancaster LW546: official records state, "disappeared without trace". (There has been much confusion re this operation mostly because researchers in the U.S have mixed the date up, it was on 6/8/1944 (August 6th) which they interpreted as the 8th of June!)

"Form up, Follow me" Pathfinder Lancaster leading the way

Copyright, Fine Art America

Godwin, Lewis John, Sergeant 590507, the Royal Air Force, died on 28/02/1941 age 27.

Son of Charles and Winifred Godwin of Abingdon, Berks. He is buried at the Capuccini Naval Cemetery, Malta. There is one other R.A.F casualty buried here, Pilot Officer Hubert Scadeng of the RAF (they are the only two members of the RAF to be buried here in the Royal Naval cemetery). This was at the height of the siege of Malta and the only aircraft based there were a small number of Gloster Gladiator Bi-Planes (two man crew) plus whatever the Fleet Air Arm could supply from the two Aircraft Carriers assigned to defend the island and related convoys. My thoughts are these two airmen were shot down while defending the island in their Gladiator Bi-plane? Toward the end of the siege there were only three Gladiator aircraft left and the islanders affectionately named them Faith, Hope & Charity, of those three only Faith survived the war and is on display at the War Museum, Valletta.

To commemorate the heroics of F. H. & Charity the first three RAF Phantom aircraft to land on the Falkland Islands after the conflict were named Faith, Hope & Charity!

The Gloster Gladiator N5520 named "Faith"

(Some facts about Malta:- there were 3,343 air raids amounting to 2,357 hours of bombing, 15,000 tons were dropped on Malta, 600 civilian casualties, 7,500 military casualties, 241 enemy aircraft shot down with a further 48 unconfirmed)

McIntyre, George, Sergeant 136057 of the Royal Air Force Volunteer Reserves, husband of Betty May McIntyre of Abingdon, Berks, Sergeant McIntyre was a gunner/wireless operator in Wellington Bombers with 21 OTU, Moreton-in-the-Marsh and died on 16/02/1942 somewhere in North Africa aged 21.

Although 21 OTU was primarily involved with night flight training new recruits, 21 OTU occasionally carried out "operational sorties" with their newly qualified airmen and were often tasked with ferrying new aircraft to various locations throughout Europe and the Middle East.

In early 42 the siege of both Malta and Tobruk were at their heights with Wellington Bombers in continuous use supporting ground troops against Rommel's Afrika corps, as well as escort duty for allied convoys through the Mediterranean.

Originally buried near his crash site in the desert he was re-buried at Massicault Cemetery some 30 kms south west of Tunis on 27th of April 1944.

This is a copy of the re-burial certificate with Sgt McIntyre top of the list. Worryingly, there is a question mark against the deceased they were reburying as to whether he was in the RAF. There is no service number listed, the surname is spelt differently and there is no date of death given.

Worrying, too, is the third entry (re-buried on the same day) that is listed as being "Unknown."

Which begs the question, "Is this really the grave of Sgt G McIntyre?"

GRAVES CONCENTRATION REPORT FORM

Report No. 22 | Schedule No. ______

Place of Burial MASSICAULT MILITARY CEMETERY.

Map Reference Tunisia, 1/50000, Series 4225, Sheet 20, 843.448.

The following are buried here :- Area No 13.

Regiment	Army No.	Name and Initials	Rank	Date of Death	Previously Buried at	Re-buried at	Date of Re-burial	Plot	Row	Grave
R.A.F. ?		MACINTYRE			8GR/FM/2039	Massicault Mil Cem	27.4.44	3	F	5
	2984664) 2987664)	BURNETT, WILLIAMS.		21.11.42	do	do	do	3	F	2
R.A.F.		UNKNOWN OFFICER			do	do	do	3	F	4
69 Sqn, RAAF.	AUS/404018	LAWRENCE, D.L.J.	Sgt	13.8.41	do	do	do	3	F	3
	4031101	OWENS,	L/Cpl		8GR/WEL/2002	do	10.5.44	4	L	12
Lothians	7951417	CRAWFORD, W.	Tpr	23.4.43	do	do	do	4	L	13
	7045512	PURDY, J.		25.4.43	do	do	do	4	L	14
R.H.A. Fd Bty.		PUCKLE,	Major	29.4.43	8GR/WEW/2005	do	do	4	L	15
2nd R.B.	..6375	CLERIHEW, C.H.P.	Lieut	29.4.43	do	do	do	4	L	16
		CHALLINOR			8GR/WEL/2002	do	do	4	L	17
R.A.F. V.R.	108813	O'BRIEN, H.P.	P/O	23.4.43	8GR/WEW/2005	do	do	4	L	18
Queens Bays	773726	SMITH, C.W.	Sgt	24.4.43	8GR/FM/2051	do	11.5.44	4	L	19
" "	7902755	TERRY, J.	Tpr	do	do	do	11.5.44	4	L	19 }
" "	3970747	NEWBOLD, F.	Tpr	do	do	do	11.5.44	4	L	19 }
R. IR. F.	7047643	TURNER, R.A.	Fus	21.1.43	8GR/FM/2053	do	12.5.44	4	J	11
1/Recce Corps	5494203	CUTLER, R.F.	L/Sgt	11.5.43	8GR/FM/2054	do	do	4	L	20

'I was present throughout the process of exhumation and have observed the order contained in Letter No Z/881/GR Dated 2 Oct 43'.

(F. McINTOSH), Capt.
No 8 Graves Registration Unit.

PSS/NA/11/43-7,000—AFHQ Press 730

Randall, Graham Donald, Sergeant 1170645 of 156 Sqn Royal Air Force Volunteer Reserve. Son of George & Edith Randall of Abingdon, Berks. Died on 16/04/1942 age 20.

Sergeant Randall was a gunner/wireless operator when on the night of the 15/04/1942 at 23.15 he and his crew mates took off from RAF Alconbury in their Wellington Bomber X3687, they crossed the channel and headed for the German town of Dortmund. It would appear his aircraft was shot down on the return leg and crashed near the town of West Viaanoerem. Of the 152 aircraft that took off for this raid 111 were Wellingtons, 19 Hampdens, 15 Stirling's and 7 Manchester's. 3 Wellington's and 1 Stirling were lost. He is buried at Vlissegem Churchyard, Belgium, along with six of his crew mates.

Trinder, Percy Donald, A/C 1 – 1313007 of the Royal Air Force (VR) son of Percy & Maud Trinder of Abingdon "died of wounds" along with A.C.1 James Rhodes of 2811 Sqn RAF Regiment. The role of the RAF Regiment was primarily to protect airfields and installations and the squadron was continuously on the move, it's not clear if they died as a result of a flying incident or "on the ground"? A.C Trinder is buried in the New Cemetery, Abingdon.

Rowe, Geoffrey William, Sergeant (pilot) 925497 of 150 Sqn the Royal Air Force Volunteer Reserve, died on the 11/05/1941 age 25, son of John and Emily Rowe, Ventnor, I of W and is buried along with four of his crew mates in Becklingen War cemetery, Germany.

At the date of his death 150 was a Wellington Bomber Sqn (which for a short period was based at R.A.F Abingdon) Wellingtons, being part of Bomber Command carried out nightly operations deep into Germany and it was on one of those missions (Hamburg) his aircraft, Wellington R1435, H-JN was listed in squadron records as "failed to return".

Luftwaffe pilot Johann Schonherr claimed he shot down R1435 at 0335 over the North Sea.

Extracts from the Isle of Wight Mercury, Friday 16th of May 1941 reported Sgt – Pilot G.W. Rowe.

"On Monday morning Mr & Mrs J.G Rowe of Alexandra Gardens received official information their eldest son, Pilot Sgt Geoffrey William was missing during operations over Germany. Prior to joining the Royal Air Force Sgt Rowe had worked for the Ventnor Urban District Council as an accountant, then, with the knowledge he gained took a post with Abingdon Urban District Council where he took on "a responsible position".

Mr & Mrs Rowe's younger son, Edwin, is also serving in the RAF as a wireless operator presently in the Middle East.

Yesterday Mr Rowe received a letter from Geoffrey's Wing Commander who, apart from offering his condolences stated that while not wishing to raise their hopes too much, but given no body has yet been found it is conceivable Geoffrey was taken prisoner?"

Tragically his brother Edwin, of 101 Sqn, died on 21/09/1942 age 23. Both are remembered on the Isle of Wight war memorial.

This is Wellington Bomber R1435 code H-JN, the aircraft Pilot G W Rowe was shot down in, to the left is Wing Commander Grant, is GW Rowe to the right?

Saunders, Reginald William, Aircraftsman 1st Class, 750305 died on the 23/04/1945 age 26. Son of Albert and Clara Saunders of Abingdon, Berks and is buried in the Labuan War Cemetery, Malaysia. After the fall of Singapore several British and Australian prisoners of war were sent to camps in Borneo. Later in anticipation of allied landings in February 1945 the Japanese decided to move these prisoners. More than 1900 British and Australian servicemen were forced to take part in the Death march from Sadakan to Ranau, those too ill to take part or who fell sick or injured en-route were simply shot or bayonetted in their sick beds. The 260 who completed the march were forced to perform superhuman work on starvation diets and of those original 1900 service men only SIX survived the war by escaping and being cared for by tribesmen. In the spring of 1945 the horror of what was happening in these death camps became known to the Allies and a planned air assault by Australian paratroopers was scheduled to take place but had to be abandoned through lack of accurate intelligence. It is reported the remaining 30 or so servicemen who were still alive in that camp were shot twelve days after the war had ended. Many hundreds of allied servicemen are scattered throughout Borneo in unmarked graves, what's more the task of identifying them was made worse by Japanese Lieutenant-Colonel Suga destroying all records and rather than face a war crime tribunal he committed suicide!

West, Harry Charles, Sergeant 1852331 of 15 Sqn, the Royal Air Force Volunteer Reserve. Died on the 15/02/1944 age 30, son of Henry and Lucy West of Titchfield, Hampshire.

15 Sqn was reformed at R.A.F Abingdon in 1934. September 1939 the Sqn flew to France flying Fairey Battle bombers, the following year it re-equipped with Blenheim's, then Wellington's before finally being equipped with Avro Lancaster's. On the night of the 15/02/1944, 891 aircraft including Lancaster's, Wellington's and Halifax bombers took off, their target was Berlin, it was the biggest raid on Berlin of the war so far and this is the Squadron record of Sergeant West's flight aboard Lancaster ED 628.

"Operation Berlin. 15/16th of February 1944 – at 1725 Lancaster ED 628 code LS-O took off Mildenhall with 13 other aircraft – at approx 2230 ED 628 shot down over Baltic - All Seven crew (including Sgt West) missing presumed dead.

All are remembered on the Runnymede Royal Air Force memorial

Luftwaffe ace Paul Zorner who claimed he shot down Lancaster ED 628

Chapter Six

Wiggins, Alan Charles, Flying Officer (pilot) 153253 of 21 Sqn the Royal Air Force Volunteer Reserve, died on 29/09/1944 age 22, son of Harry and Julia Wiggins of Abingdon, Berks.

F/O Wiggins is buried at Leopoldsburg War Cemetery, Belgium. This cemetery was used for burials from many of the German military hospitals in the area as well as allied RAF personnel who "didn't make it back".

At that time 21 was a Mosquito Sqn and the Mosquito was famous for the daring daylight raid on the Philips factory and operation Jericho when Mosquitos attacked a Gestapo prison camp holding up to 200 resistance fighters that intelligence had reported were about to be executed. The attack breached the prison walls and many of its inmates escaped!

There are some serious misgivings about how F/O Wiggins (navigator) and his crew mate F/O George MacCleod (Pilot) met their deaths in Mosquito NT179 on the return leg of their mission to Dusseldorf and "the cover up" that followed it? Not long after their demise official records stated they was shot down by a Junkers 88, however, approaching the end of the war there was an inquiry into the event and an eye witness (a young girl) came forward who not only saw the Mosquito being shot down, but was first on the scene of the crash. Once there she had the presence of mind to take down the names of the two dead crew men, shortly after members of the resistance arrived and recovered the two bodies from the wreck, they buried them in a shallow grave on the grass verge and stood guard over them for a few days until they were officially recovered. Importantly she was adamant they were shot down by another Mosquito, not a Junkers 88?

Mindful of the witness statement re being shot down by another Mosquito the relatives pressed the MOD for further investigation, however the MOD claimed to have inspected the flight log of the only other squadron operating Mosquitos anywhere near that vicinity which stated categorically there were no Mosquitos operating near the shooting down of F/O Wiggins plane?

About 2006 a group of Belgium amateur aviation historians picked up the story and began by visiting the crash site and unbelievable made contact with the then young girl eye witness. Now Madame De Keyser who took the historians to the crash site and went over the events of the night, adamant it was a Mosquito, not a Junkers that did the deed? Believing in their witness they began trawling over squadron logs and flight history of aircraft operating in that area and concluded it was more than likely they were shot down by Mosquito HK250 of 219 Sqn, but more unbelievable they concluded the squadron log for that day had been deliberately "doctored" so as to give the location of HK250 nowhere near the location of the shot down Mosquito! (RAF/MOD took very seriously any hint of friendly fire casualties and it was known that records were deliberately altered so as to cover up any such incident)

Apparently too there was a "Ground Control Interception" mobile radar team operating in that area and all RAF aircraft gave out an identification code which was picked up by this radar identifying them as friendly, but ironically the crew (and this was their first ever sortie together) had not switched the device on and given they were flying at a height and at a location not normally used by returning aircraft they were assumed to be hostile.

The historians raised funds enough to begin a salvage operation of NT179 and the enigma may have been finally solved with a letter from the pilot of the rouge Mosquito HK250 to a relative of one of the airmen in which he apparently suggested he may have shot down NT179 mistaking it for Junkers 88!

I was never aware of the identities of the crew of the Mosquito or of the Sqn involved, but now with that knowledge, this matter takes a much more personal aspect. Over the years it troubled me from time to time, but I'm afraid I never did anything about it, and I suppose the passage of time eased my conscience. As far as I know, no one other than the service personnel of that period knew anything about this matter until now. Certainly not my family, it was not the sort of thing one talked about. I have never been great on correspondence and have found this letter very difficult to write.

What can I say after all these years except that I am so very sorry that my action in 1944 resulted in the deaths of those two young men and undoubtedly caused a lot of anguish and grief to their families and friends.

I cannot think of anything else to add, but you now have my address and I will only be too willing to help if anything further is needed to close out this tragic affair.

Yours Sincerely
"Withheld"
pilot of HK250.

Conclusive evidence Mosquito NT179 was shot down by Mosquito HK250 and that there was a deliberate attempt to cover up that tragic incidence.

Photograph of 21 Squadron pilots & crew 1944, are F/O's Wiggins & MacCleod there?

A prayer for our airmen written by Noel Coward

Lie in the dark and listen. It's clear tonight so they're flying high, Hundreds of them, thousands perhaps, riding the icy, moonlit sky.

Men, machinery, bombs and maps, Altimeters, guns and charts, Coffee, sandwiches, fleece-lined boots,

Bones and muscles and minds and hearts, English saplings with English roots

Deep in the earth they've left below. Lie in the dark and let them go; Lie in the dark and listen. Lie in the dark and listen.

They're going over in waves and waves High above villages, hills and streams, Country churches and little graves

And little citizens worried dreams; Very soon they'll have reached the sea and far below them will lie the bays

And cliffs and sands where they used to be taken for summer holidays. Lie in the dark and let them go; theirs is a world we'll never know.

Lie in the dark and listen. Lie in the dark and listen.

City magnates and steel contractors Factory workers and politicians Soft hysterical little actors, Ballet dancers, reserved musicians

Safe in your warm civilian beds, Count your profits and count your sheep Life is passing above your heads,

Just turn over and try to sleep. Lie in the dark and let them go, there's one debt you'll forever owe,

Lie in the dark and listen.

Chapter Seven

Commonwealth War Graves of WW2 servicemen Buried in Abingdon Cemeteries

The Royal Air Force

At the beginning of WW2, Royal Air Force Abingdon was to have been a training base made up of two squadrons, 97 & 166 (from Leconfield) with 12 Armstrong-Whitworth Whitely Bombers and 4 Avro Anson trainers. RAF Abingdon then morphed into 10 Operational Training Unit (OTU) and became very much an operational airfield dispatching heavy bombers on their nightly raids across Europe as well as the later 1,000 aircraft sorties instigated by Bomber Command. RAF Abingdon endured its first air raid by the Luftwaffe on 3rd of December 1940 at about 1700 hrs, six bombs were dropped damaging the officers mess. Three further attacks were made on the base on the evenings of the 12/14 & 21st of March 1941, during the attacks, bombs were dropped on Shippon Church and on Evelin Road too. RAF Abingdon had an assortment of aircraft stationed here during WW2, Halifax, Wellington, Whitley, Anson and Hind to name but a few and many of which crashed on or near the airfield! Sadly, some of those airmen based at RAF Abingdon, in one way or another lost their lives and fourteen have been buried here in Commonwealth War Grave Commission graves across three cemeteries, The Original Cemetery Road site, the "new cemetery" at Spring Gardens and two burials in the Roman Catholic Church of Saint Edmund.

Abingdon Whitley Bomber

Copyright, google images

Costello, Maurice Henry, wireless operator 546959, 166 Sqn and based at RAF Abingdon, died on 08/04/1940.

Davies, John Middleton, Pilot Officer 40594 166 Sqn, based at RAF Abingdon also died on 08/04/1940. On the 8th of April 1940 Whitley bomber K8957 took off from RAF Abingdon as part of 10 OTU (operational training unit) unfortunately the aircraft, suffering the effects of severe icing crashed at Long Marston. The crew who died in the accident were: - F/O AL McSherry, P/O KR Ainsworth, *L.A.C. MH Costello* *P/O JM Davies,* however P/O GW Salzgeber managed to parachute to safety. He later changed his name to Salter?

Robinson, Clair, P/O 75171 of 97 Sqn, based at RAF Abingdon. P/O Robinson was killed on the 18/12/1939 when his Whitley Bomber K7620 took off from RAF Abingdon, but crashed soon after at Kingston Bagpuize. Of the crew of three F/O 39526 JG Howard also died and is buried at Kingston

Bagpuize church cemetery, on board too was Sgt A Cowe, I cannot find him listed as a casualty, so assume he survived?

Bligh, Orley, P/o 42186 of 97 Sqn based at RAF Abingdon died on the 10th of February 1940 aged 24 when his Whitley Bomber K7255 crashed at Boars Hill, Wootton, P/O Bligh is the son of William & Mary Bligh of Berwick, Nova Scotia, Canada. His crew mate Sgt/Pilot 517894 Reginald Frederick Cyril Dupe also died and is buried at St Stephens Church, Lympne.

Hunter, Harry Blakeway, Pilot officer (air gunner) 77208 of 166 Sqn based at RAF Abingdon died on 12th of March 1940 age 19, son of Mr & Mrs Thomas Hunter of Leicester. Whitley Bomber K8960 crashed into the officer's mess at RAF Abingdon on 12/03/1940 at 11.45 am killing the crew of three. Civilian casualties are listed as one dead and five injured.

Ray, Norman, Flt Sgt 517749 died on 01/08/1942, Flt Sgt Ray was based at RAF Abingdon and at the time of his death there was only one aircraft lost that could be attributed to him? Whitely Bomber Z6562 was involved in a "flying accident" on the airfield?

McKee, Patrick, Sgt W/op Air Gunner 911283 RAF VR of 10 OTU RAF Abingdon, the son of Mr Percy & Eleanor McKee of Worthing, Sussex, died on 11th of October 1940 age 21. Whitley Bomber N1526 took off from RAF Abingdon on a routine night training exercise but crashed near the landing strip at Akerman Street killing all the crew of six, the cause of the crash is given as a large area of fabric came unattached from the main frame. Sgt McKee is buried in a CWGC grave in the Catholic Cemetery of Saint Edmunds Church.

Trinder Percy Donald. A.C.1.1313007, Royal Air Force (VR) son of Percy & Maud Trinder of Abingdon. Died 16th November 1942. A.C 1 Trinder "died of wounds" along with A.C1 James Rhodes of 2811 Sqn RAF regiment. The role of the RAF Regiment was primarily to protect airfields. The Sqn continuously travelled around from location to location, it's not clear if they were killed "on the ground" or as a result of an air crash? A.C Trinder is remembered on the Abingdon War memorial.

Fairey Battle

Copyright, google images

Bennett, Herbert Bapume, A.C.1 620296 of 13 OTU unit (training) was based at RAF Bicester, he died on the 10th of June 1940 aged 23 and was the husband of Edith May Bennett of Abingdon. A.C Bennett was on board Fairey Battle aircraft that was involved in a flying accident, his crew mates, Flt Lt (pilot) Alan Chalmers and AC2 Samuel Davis were also killed. A.C 1 Bennett is remembered on the Abingdon war Memorial.

Rhind, Geoffrey Arthur Cyril. Pilot Officer 41322 of 35 Sqn based at RAF Abingdon. Died on 29th October 1939. While on a training flight in his Fairey Battle aircraft K9472, making a final approach to Carew, Cheriton when the aircraft flew into a cliff killing all on board. His crew mates were A/C, E W Looker and A/C, B Connor.

Avro Anson

Copyright, google images

Collins, Vincent, LAC 1182779 of the 11th Air Observers Navigation School, RAF, son of Mr & Mrs James Collins and husband of Mary from Streatham, London, died on 7th of June 1941 age 33. LAC Collins died when his Anson N9735 crashed on a training flight. LAC Collins is buried in a CWGC grave in the Catholic cemetery, Saint Edmunds Church, Abingdon

Ralph, Joe, Pilot Officer (pilot) 41463 of 15 Sqn based at RAF Abingdon, son of Mr & Mrs George Ralph of Hove, Sussex. Died on 30th September 1939 age 19. While flying in Hawker Hind K5373 from RAF Abingdon the aircraft hit "high ground" 2 m north of Cranwell killing Plt/Off George Habgood age 20 and Plt/Off Joe Ralph age 19. Plt/Off Habgood is buried in his home town at Faringdon church.

This is believed to be the funeral (with honours) of Plt/Off Joe Ralph, Abingdon cemetery?

Hawker Hind

Walker, Leslie Edward, Sgt Air Gunner 1852244 RAF VR died on the 8th of September 1944 age 19, Sgt Walker is the son of Mr Thomas & Mrs Beatrice Walker of Boars Hill Abingdon.

As part of 29 OTU, Wellington Bomber BK552 (sign F for Freddy) took off from its base at RAF Bruntingthorpe on 8th September 1944 for a pre-set navigation training exercise.

However, two hours into the flight, with both engines suffering from severe icing, the Wellington crashed killing all crew. They were: - Pilot F/O De-Villiers Clark, Nav P/O H Holmes, Nav 2 Sgt Gordon Manning, W/Op Sgt Clifford Taylor. Gunner, Sgt Thomas Donovan Potter (RAAF) Gunner Sgt John Nicholson, and Air Gunner Sgt, Lesley Walker.

The training flight route of BK552

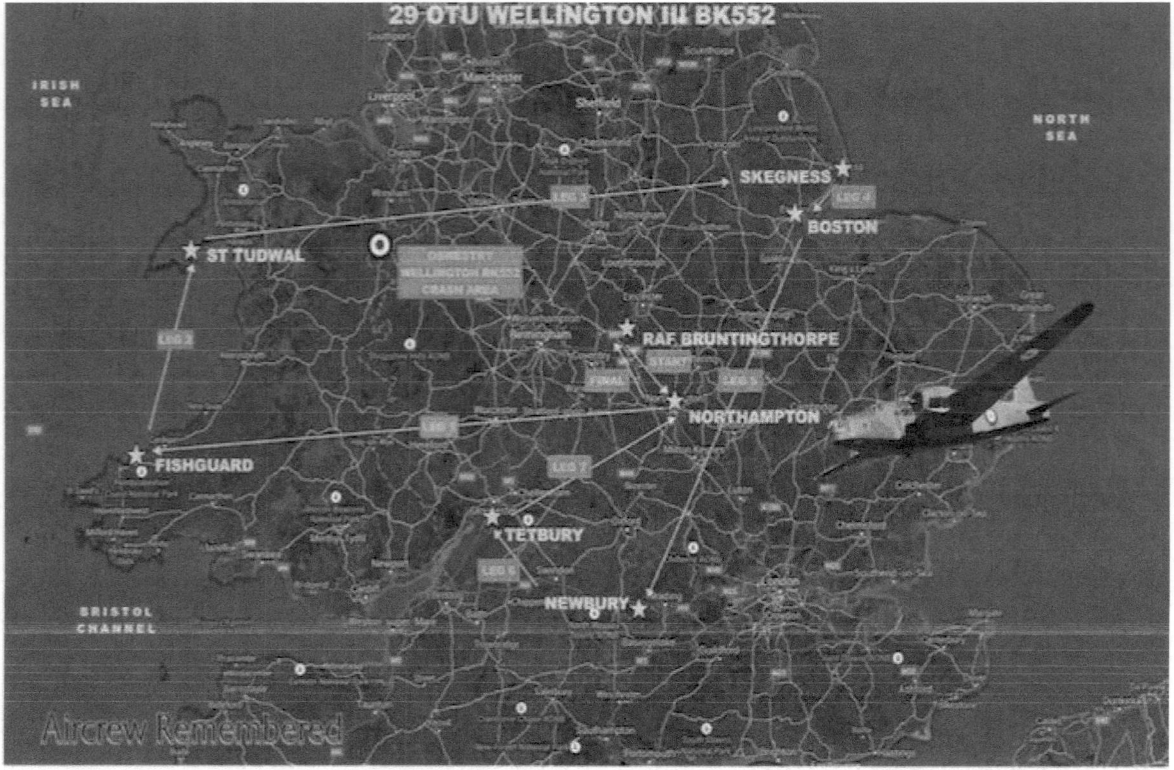

EVIDENCE 1st Witness.

F/L. Robert Burr.
29. O.T.U. being duly sworn states;-

I am deputy flight commander at 29. O.T.U. BRUNTINGTHORPE. On the 8th September 1944 I was detailed to brief crews for day cross country Base NORTHAMPTON - FISHGUARD - ST TUDWAL'S SKEGNESS BOSTON NEWBURY TETBURY NORTHAMPTON - BASE. F/O. D CLARKE and full crew were present. SGT MANNING was also detailed to actvas second navigator in the aircrafts crew. The aircraft was WELLINGTON MK.III BK552 (F).

Before commencement of briefing I consulted the Meteorological Officer and was given the following forecast for the route. Heavy Cu and Cu Nim would be building up with base in the region of 3500feet main tops at 15000 feet but with isolated tops up to 20000 to 22000 feet. Icing index would be high in this cloud. Thundery showers would develop later. In view of this and also being warned by the O.C. Flying S/L. E.S. KENNEDY A.F.C., I suppervised specialist briefing and then held main briefing. Here I gave the following specific instructions :- All crews were to climb above the cloud and fly above it throughout the route, they were to fly around the isolated tops, if they were unable to fly above or around the cloud, they were to return to base. When the captains reported later to sign the authorisation book I re-emphasised the importance of not flying in cloud, with special reference to those flying WELLINGTON MK III aircraft in view of their lower operational height.

Aircrew Remembered

(Sgd.). R. Burr. F/Lt. (S

Copyright aircrew remembered

Ironically, aircraft (BK552) was, on December 29th 1943, at R.A.F Bitteswell, involved in a collision with Wellington X3872. Neither aircraft were seriously damaged, however the bomb aimer (positioned in the very front) in BK552, 21 year old Wallace Blakely of the RCAF was killed.

Wellington Bomber

Halifax Bomber

Copyright, airvectors.net

Dockerty, Bradford William, Flt Sgt 1801212 of 640 Bomber Sqn, RAF VR, son of Mr & Mrs AH Dockerty of Send, Surrey. Died on 02/02/1945 age 21 and is buried in the new cemetery, Abingdon. On the night of 2nd of February 1945 the crew of Halifax MZ 492 took off from RAF Leconfield at 20.36 hrs to bomb the oil refinery at Wanna-Eickel and was this crew's first operational sortie.

Shortly after take it is believed the aircraft took a sharp turn to the left, apparently to miss a church steeple, however, the aircraft stalled and lost height, then struck a tree and crashed killing all but one of the crew, they were :- Pilot 425979 Noel Sisley, age 20 of the Royal Australian Air Force, from Wooloowin, Queensland, he is buried at Harrogate cemetery. Flight Engineer 3030814 Sqt Peter Jefferies RAF VR, age 19 from Bromham, F/E Jefferies is buried at Stagsden Church yard, Beds. Navigator, Sgt 1673230 Thomas Gibson, RAF VR age 21 of Bamburgh, Northumberland. Sgt Gibson is buried at Bamburgh cemetery. Bomb Aimer, Sgt 1565369 Alexander Gray, RAF VR, age 22 of Aberdeen. Sgt Gray is buried at Springbank cemetery, Aberdeen. Wireless operator/air gunner, Sgt 1683581 Martin Delahunty, RAF VR, age 21 of Prestwich. Sgt Delahunty is buried at Prestwich Cemetery, Lancashire.*Mid Upper Gunner, Flt/Sgt 1801212 Dockerty, RAF VR. Flt Sgt Dockerty is buried in the new Abingdon cemetery.* Rear Gunner, Sgt 1882495 J S Whitman, RAF VR, unbelievably survived unscathed!

Williams, Arthur Hamilton W/O 358652 died on 04/06/1942, age 45, Warrant Officer Williams is the husband of Katherine Williams of Abingdon. W/O Williams died of natural causes at the Princess Mary Military Hospital, RAF Halton. W/O Williams is not remembered on the Abingdon War memorial?

Chapter Eight

The Royal Navy

Thomas, Kenneth, A/S P/JX322128 of HMS Scylla, The Royal Navy, the son of Arthur & Kate Thomas of Abingdon, died on February 12th 1944 age 20.

In September of 43 HMS Scylla was in support of the defence of Malta but later in the month suffered damage to her turbines and withdrew to Chatham naval base on the river Medway for repairs. She was in Chatham from October 43 until March 44 when her next duties were to take a leading role in the D-Day invasion. Able Seaman Thomas service number prefix P/JX suggests he was in the Royal Marines, Chatham was a major RM base.

During WW2 there were over 1,300 air raid alerts over the Medway resulting in approximately 2,783 high explosives and 24,421 incendiary bombs being dropped there as well as a small number of "flying bombs" resulting in 187 deaths and 1,096 injuries, given his ship was in dock here the assumption is he died in a raid on his RM camp there? A/S Thomas is not remembered on the Abingdon War Memorial?

HMS Scylla survives a hole in her deck after a glider bomb attack

Copyright, ww2today.com

Hemmings, Kenneth, W R, Ordinary Seaman P/JX21543 died on the 05/12/1940, son of William and Kate Hemmings of Abingdon, Berks. O/S Hemmings served at HMS Excellent which was a training establishment in Portsmouth, He is buried at Abingdon Cemetery.

1940 was the beginning of the Blitz (and the battle of Britain) and Portsmouth was particularly singled out because of its naval importance. One of the first "city-wide" air raids on Portsmouth took place on December the 5th (the day of Kenneth's death) there were 40 reported fatalities and about 140 casualties, based on this information it is probable that Kenneth was among those forty fatalities killed in the air raid? O/S Hemmings is remembered on the Abingdon War Memorial.

Sellwood, Alfred Francis, Petty Officer P/J 114222 of HMS Egret, The Royal Navy, died on 7th of February 1942, husband of Mrs EE Sellwood of Gosport.

Curiously I can find no mention of HMS Egret being in any specific action on or prior to the date of death?

However, in 1942 the West Africa Station was set up in the port of Freetown, Sierra Leone. It was predominantly a naval base (with marine garrison) tasked to provide safe escort of ships en-route to and from the Cape to the GB.

HMS Egret was stationed there during this time as one of the escort ships. Quite why he was buried at Abingdon is mysterious?

Chapter Nine

The Army

Belcher, Percy, Pte 5333831 of the Army catering Corps attached to the 4th battalion, The Royal Berkshire Regiment died May 9th 1942 age 29. After the 4th Royal Berks were all but wiped out at Dunkirk the remnants of the Battalion was stationed on the Isle of Thanet, Kent which was also home to RAF Manston as well as the ports of Ramsgate, Margate and Dover all of which made the area a prime target for the Luftwaffe. At the time of his death the Nazi's launched Operation Baedeker, which was a concerted effort on specific targets rather than indiscriminate blanket bombing. The idea was to destroy buildings and infrastructure in an attempt to lower moral and the spirit of the civilian population, Thanet took a particular, almost nightly pounding through the months of April & May and it is believed Pte Belcher was killed in one such raid? Pte P Belcher is remembered on the Abingdon War Memorial.

Belcher, William Edward, Saper 14398672 of 5 Bomb Disposal Company, the Royal Engineers, son of Edward & Mary Belcher of Abingdon died on 22nd of March 1945 age 36. Originally 5 BDC were based in Nottingham and London, but on 5th of July 1944 they sailed from Southampton to Arromanches in support of the Normandy invasions and were then based at Coulombs. France, from where they worked their way forward. Saper Belcher is remembered on the Abingdon War Memorial.

Short, Arthur Albert, Pte 5339032 of the 4th Battalion The Royal Berkshire Regiment, son of William & Fanny Short and husband to Violet of Abingdon, died on the 22nd of February 1942 age 41.

Given the 4th Battalion were based on the Isle of Thanet (see Pte Belcher above) I'm assuming he died in one of the many air raids to that area? Pte Short is remembered on the Abingdon War Memorial.

Gawthorne, Arthur Joseph, Pte 7630926 of the Royal Ordinance Corps, husband of Marguerite Lillian Gawthorne of Abingdon died on the 7th of October 1940.

The Royal Ordinance Corps was responsible for the supply and maintenance of weapons, munitions and vehicles and operated from bases/camps throughout the country, although I can find no place of death and this was at the height of the Blitz I'm assuming he was killed in an air raid? Pte Gawthorne is remembered on the Abingdon War Memorial.

Giles, Thomas, Gunner 1675412 of 514 Battery, 83rd Search Light Regiment, The Royal Artillary, died on the 17th November 1943.

The 83rd SLR were originally based in Crewe, however, In August 1943 the 83rd were transferred to Kent and came under the control of Biggin Hill sector which at the time was under almost daily attack by the Luftwaffe.

Their search light was also fitted with Browning 0.5 inch machine guns and was radar operated. My thoughts are Gunner Giles died in an air raid?

Mobile radar-assisted search light

Copyright, google images

Jakeman, Cyril Arthur, Cpt 83206 M.C. formerly of the 1st Berkshire (Abingdon) Btn Home Guard. Cpt Jakeman M.C. died on the 25th of December 1943 (Christmas day) age 47, Son of George & Clare Jakeman and husband of Hilda Doreen Jakeman J.P of Abingdon. There is an obituary about Capt Jakeman written by Critchleys & Co, an accountancy firm in Abingdon dated February 1944. Given his age he would have qualified for WW1 and I'm assuming he ascended to the rank of Captain in that conflict, when WW2 broke out and was given a post in the Abingdon Home Guard, but died of natural causes while working for Critchleys as an accountant? Capt Jakeman M.C. is buried in the new Abingdon Cemetery but is not remembered on the Abingdon War Memorial?

Inspection of the Abingdon Home Guard in May 1943. Is Captain Jakeman present?

H. Evans

Chapter Ten

Operation Chariot

Earlier here I gave mention to the raid on St Nazaire? Operation Chariot is often referred to as the greatest raid of all time!

St Nazaire was of strategic importance to the German war machine in that it was the only dry dock large enough to serve as a repair/maintenance facility for the mighty German Fleet operating in the Atlantic and home seas and in particular their huge battleships.

The allies realised it had to be "taken out", Persistent bombing raids had failed to be of any significant success and so an ambitious plan to raid and destroy the facility was hatched.

The plan was to convert a royal navy war ship, HMS Campbeltown into a look-a-like German navy ship and under the cover of darkness sail it up the Loire estuary where she would be rammed into the dry dock gates, then blown sky high!

March the 27th 1942 with 265 Commandos and 346 Navy personnel on board, Campbeltown began the last part of her history. Around midnight the RAF carried out a huge bombing raid on the dock facility, this was to draw searchlights away from the sea and estuary allowing Campbeltown to slip to her target, around 0100 the RAF withdrew and Campbeltown made her final run in, she slammed into the dock gates successfully, the next part of the raid was for the 265 commandos to wreak havoc among the dock yard and although there was a "return" plan in place where-by RN ships and a submarine at sea were ready to dispatch small boats to pick up those who made it to the rendezvous point, most knew it was a one-way ticket!

Ladders off the bow of the ship were quickly put in place and the Commandos began their job.

One of the first off was well known Abingdonian. Ron Chung. Ron, a long-time family friend who went to school with my mother was at the forefront of the raid, referred to in documents as the fearless China-man, it was Ron's job to be the first around any corner and through any door, with his knife he was the silent dispatcher.

After several hours of often hand to hand combat and with most of their force either killed or had made their escape via the planned route, about 100 or so Commandos were left scattered around the docks when the order was given "every-man for himself" each man had been told prior to the raid their only escape route was to try to make for the Pyrenees and the Spanish boarder.

Ron had been shot and most were out of ammunition, soon they were overpowered by the 5000 army garrison stationed there. They were all captured! However, Campbeltown's four ton of explosives hadn't detonated, then, just as the last Commandos were being rounded up, she blew in spectacular fashion. Mission accomplished!

Thankfully Ron survived his time as a P.O.W and his part in the greatest ever raid was cemented in Commando history.

Ron Chung, (left) of 12 Commando, the Royal Marines.

Commando archives

HMS Campbeltown astride the dock gates and blown!

Uncle John & H.M.S. Norfolk

It would be unforgiveable of me to write my little book without mentioning Uncle John.

“Johnny” Carter came to Abingdon in the 1930's with his parents, when his father “Pop” Carter had been appointed Lock Keeper here. When war broke out “Pop”, previously a diver in the Royal Navy, was immediately recalled leaving Johnny and his mother in charge of the Lock, it was during that time Johnny became a member of the Upper Thames Patrol. But that was soon about to change when he volunteered to join the Royal Navy.

“Johnny” on the deck 3rd from the right as part of the Upper Thames Patrol

Thamesatwar

Out of training Johnny joined H.M.S. Norfolk as a stoker. Johnny, good looking strong as an ox, a marksman and keen rugby player soon settled into life at sea and "hot" bedding in mess 32.

As a child I remember Johnny recalling to me the various scenarios HMS Norfolk found herself in, but one such mission, to find and sink the German capital ship Scharnhorst was tearfully told.

The Scharnhorst had an impressive array of guns and at a time held the record for the longest distance shelling, she caused havoc around Norway, Iceland the North Atlantic and the supply route to Russia, (the route to Murmansk). Among her victims were HMS's Renown, Rawalpindi, the aircraft carrier Glorious as well as her escorts Acasta and Ardent. Clearly she had to go and a plan was hatched to track, (through newly acquired radar) to a suitable location and "take her on".

December 1943 and Scharnhorst was picked up heading toward the Denmark Straights, a battle group was assembled comprising the battle ship Duke of York along with the cruisers Norfolk, Belfast, Sheffield and Jamaica when early on Boxing day Scharnhorst came within range.

One of the first to close and open fire on Scharnhorst was Johnny's HMS Norfolk, her first two shells hit Scharnhorst knocking out her radar and causing damage to her bridge, but that came at a price, Scharnhorst returned fire on Norfolk scoring two direct hits with 28Cm shells killing six of Johnny's crew mates beside him.

Norfolk opens fire

Norfolk, badly damaged had to break off the engagement and limp home for repairs, while en-route Johnny's six ship mates were buried at sea. They are remembered on the Plymouth Naval memorial.

The route to Murmansk

When escorting convoys of arms and equipment through the Arctic and beyond to Russia all crew were expected to "ice chip" The weight of ice across the decks and equipment was such that it could topple the ship this photo I had developed from negatives Johnny took.

HMS Norfolk's role in WW2 was as valuable as it was numerous, she took part in sinking Bismark, Convoy PQ17, Operation Torch (invasion of North Africa) sinking U boats as well as German surface ships, like his Friend Ron Chung, Johnny survived the war too!

DID2811014

L - #0549 - 140420 - C0 - 210/148/5 - PB - DID2811014